The Layers Around Me
By Aaron Fields

ISBN: **978-1-953962-58-4**

🌸 DEVELOPMENTAL GOAL:

It's imperative that we help children understand that their world is made up of different layers—family, school, neighborhood, media, culture—and that all these things work together to shape how they feel, learn, and grow.

"Hello,

I hope all is well. I'm just a young girl.

I laugh, I dream, I cry.

But some people forget that I'm still a girl.

Still growing. Still learning.

Still needing to be held and noticed."

"The people close to me are supposed to keep me safe.

But sometimes they call me 'fast.'

Say I'm 'too grown.'

Tell me not to cry.

But I'm just a little girl."

"When I'm punished for being me,

I start to wonder-----

Is it safe to shine?"

I am
smart

I am
kind

I am
enough

"Mama tried to talk to the school.

They said, 'She's got an attitude.'

No one asked if something was wrong.

No one asked if I was okay."

"When grown-ups don't work together,

I fall between them."

"My doctor's office is always rushed.

They don't hear Mama's questions.

They don't ask me how I feel.

I learned early: speak fast, or not at all."

"Sometimes the rules are made far away------

But I still feel them deep inside."

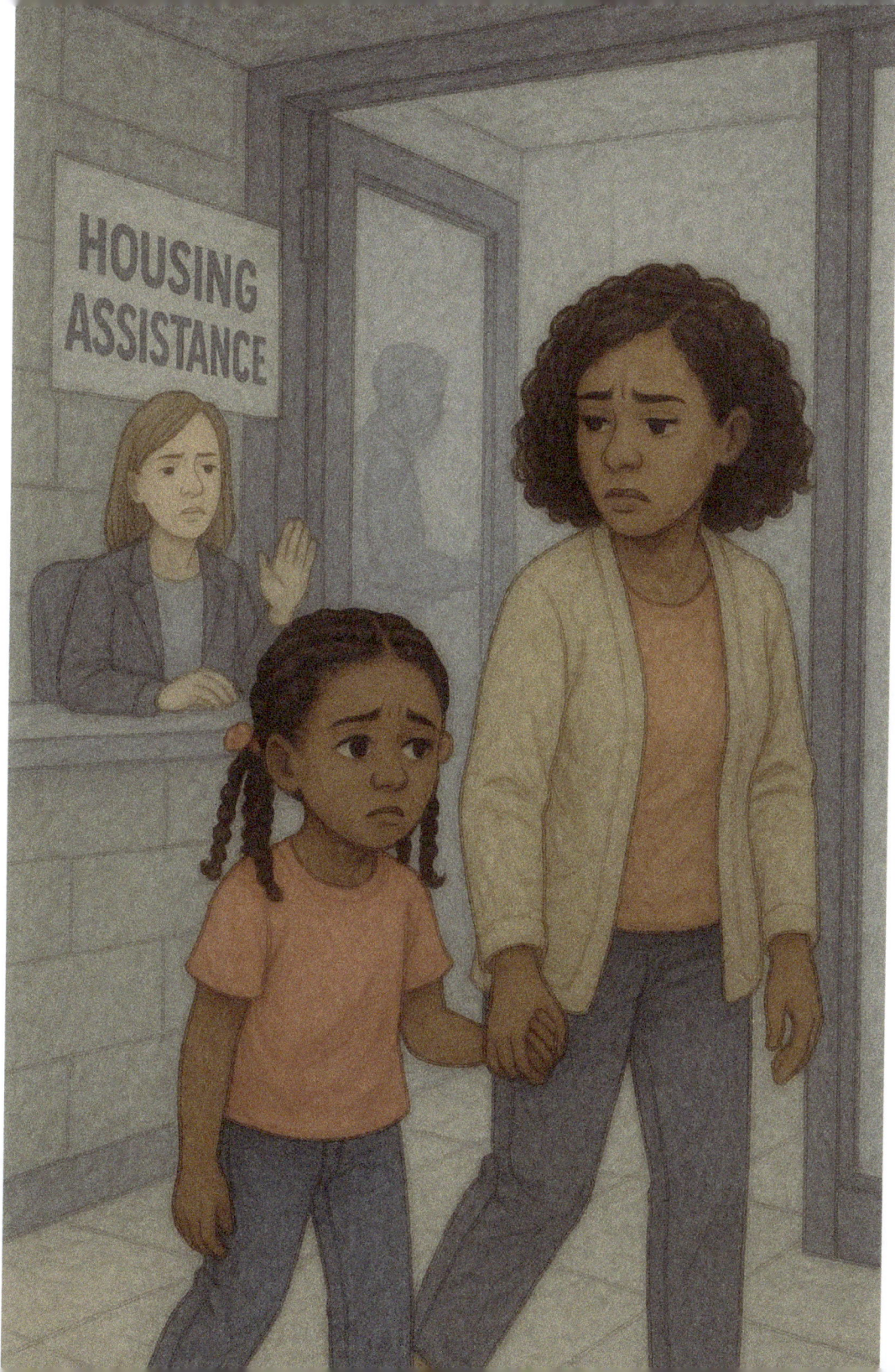

"TV says girls like me are loud.

Or magic. Or angry.

Rarely just…..regular."

"When the world only tells part of my story,

It gets harder to love all of me."

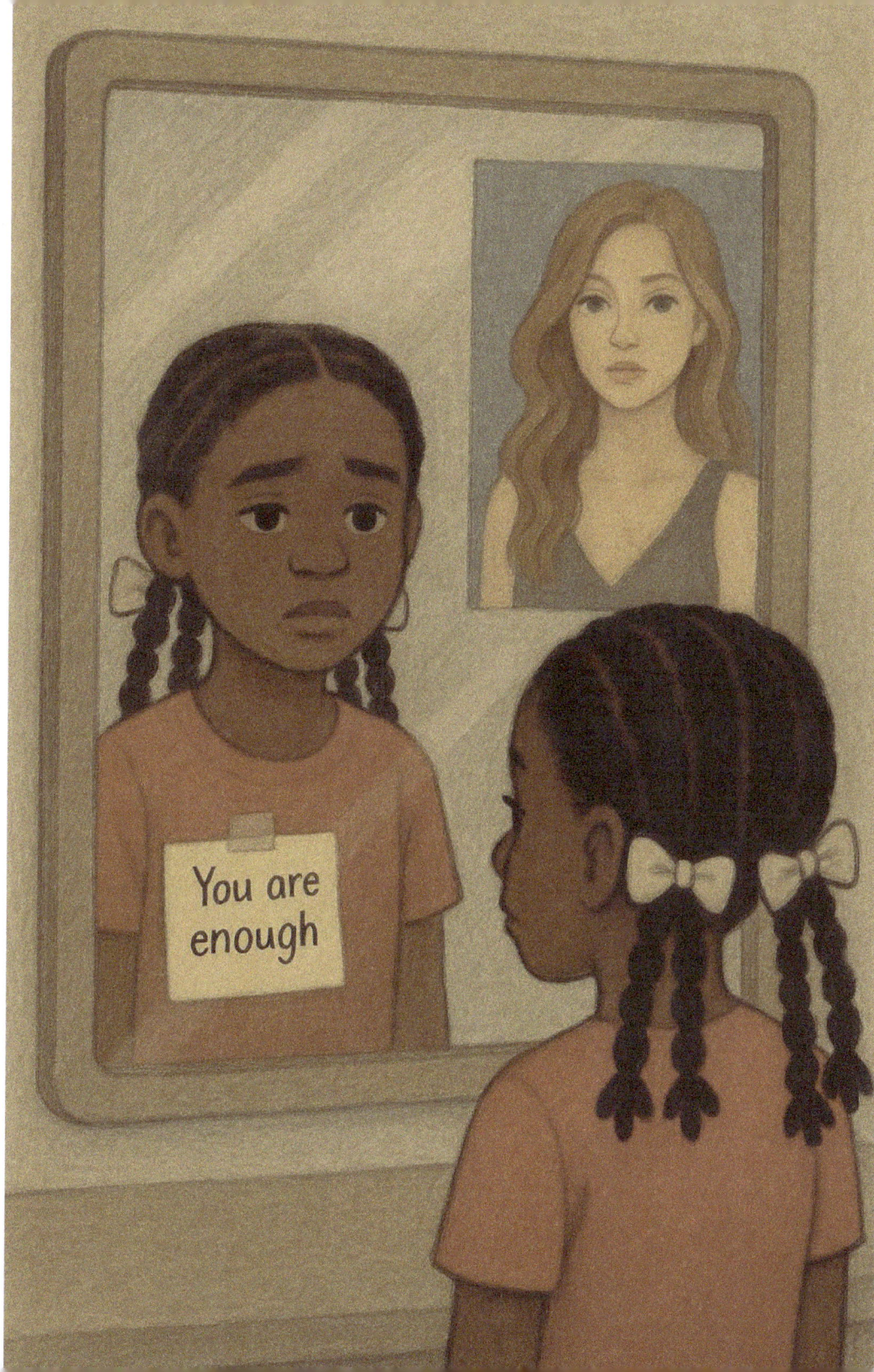

"At 4, they said I was 'too loud.'

At 6, 'too sassy.'

At 9, 'too emotional.'

What will they say when I'm 13?"

"When I carry grown-up expectations,

I don't get to be little for long."

"I carry shame that was never mine.

I carry silence.

I carry strength too early."

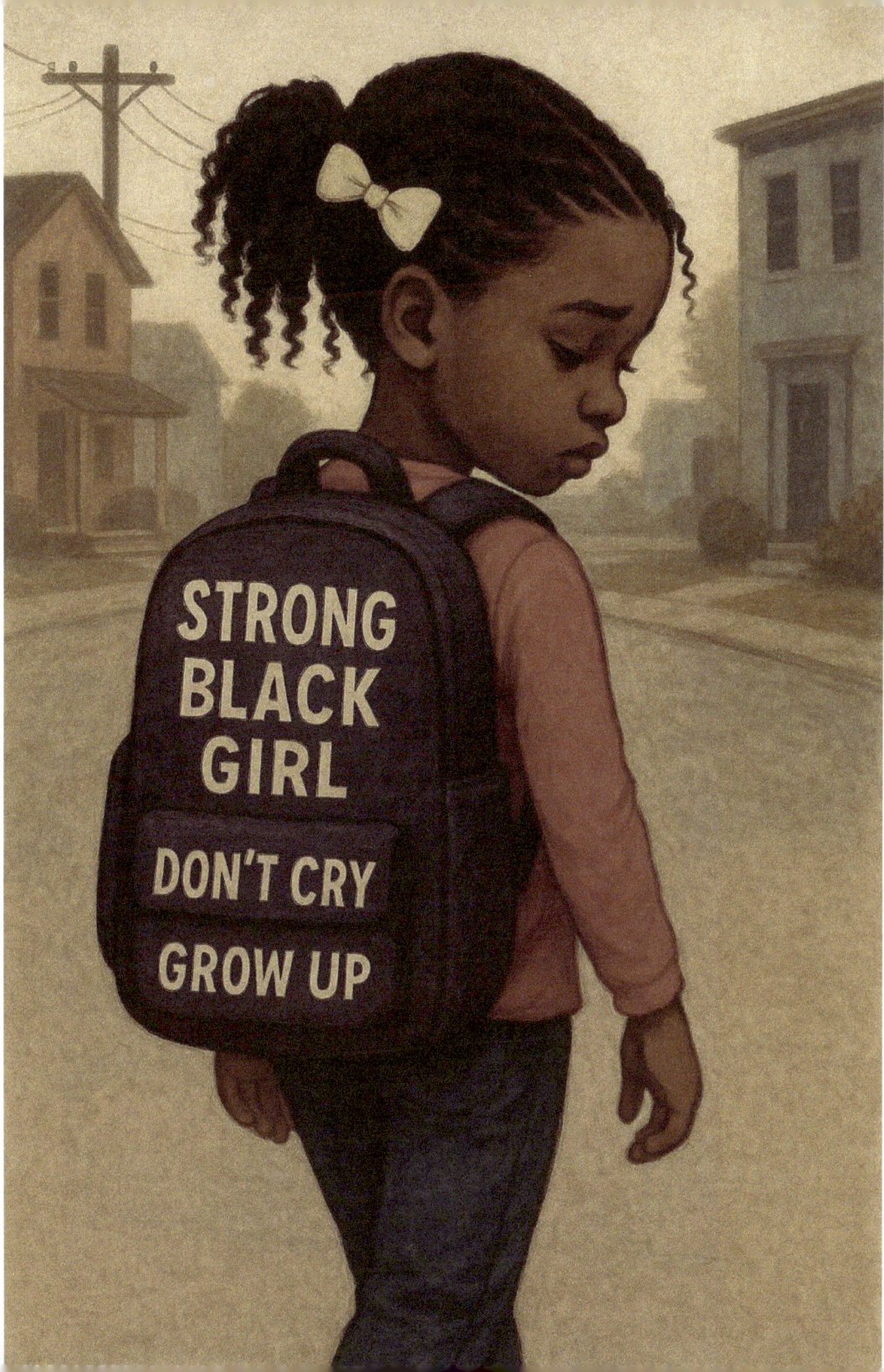

"I deserve soft.

I deserve slowness.

I deserve to be held,

Not hardened."

"My voice is not too loud.

My heart is not too much.

I'm a garden that needs gentleness to bloom."

"I am smart.

I am silly.

I am sensitive.

I am a girl.

PLEASE.....let me be little."